What Fathers Should Tell Their

Daughters

Communication Between Fathers and Daughters
About Obedience and Relationships
for Ages Ten to Eighteen

LOUISE BRUNNER

WESTBOW
P R E S S®
A DIVISION OF THOMAS NELSON
& ZONDERVAN

Scriptures taken from the Holy Bible, New International Version®, NIV®. Copyright © 1973, 1978, 1984, 2011 by Biblica, Inc.™ Used by permission of Zondervan. All rights reserved worldwide. www.zondervan.com The "NIV" and "New International Version" are trademarks registered in the United States Patent and Trademark Office by Biblica, Inc.™

WestBow Press books may be ordered through booksellers or by contacting:

WestBow Press
A Division of Thomas Nelson & Zondervan
1663 Liberty Drive
Bloomington, IN 47403
www.westbowpress.com
1 (866) 928-1240

Because of the dynamic nature of the Internet, any web addresses or links contained in this book may have changed since publication and may no longer be valid. The views expressed in this work are solely those of the author and do not necessarily reflect the views of the publisher, and the publisher hereby disclaims any responsibility for them.

Any people depicted in stock imagery provided by Thinkstock are models, and such images are being used for illustrative purposes only. Certain stock imagery © Thinkstock.

ISBN: 978-1-9736-1308-4 (sc)
ISBN: 978-1-9736-1307-7 (e)

Library of Congress Control Number: 2018900039

Print information available on the last page.

WestBow Press rev. date: 1/8/2018

Dedication

This book is dedicated to:

An answer to prayer, my two sons, have become wonderful Christian Father's whom I am well pleased. My youngest, Geoff Nikkel has four daughters to raise, Rhiannon, Kennedy, Ashlyn, and Reagan.

In addition, there is Karson whom one day may become a father and I hope this is helpful to him. Although Karson and Kennedy are not his biologically, this family is happily united, in Jesus Christ.

My oldest son, Rob Nikkel, has two daughters Ryen and Rylie. His son Reid knows Christ died on the cross for him. One day he may become a father of daughters. They are all outgoing, competitive in sports, love animals, love life, and all know the Love of Jesus Christ. What a blessing.

Both my sons couldn't do it all without the help of their lovely wives. Geoff's Abbey and Rob's Kristi so thank you Lord for all of them.

Not every young girl has a Father around but we all have our heavenly Father who wants to form a relationship with us for a lifetime.

My husband has three granddaughters Siri, Tova, and Tamaya are lovely loving children who also know the Lord. I hope this book helps them in their journey to develop a strong relationship with their heavenly Father for a lifetime.

Chapter 1

Obedience and Self-Control

And being found in appearance of a man,
He humbled himself and became obedient
to death Even death on the cross.
—Philippians 2:8

As young girls, when you start thinking of how you make decisions, do you include obedience to your father or of true obedience to your heavenly Father? Our heavenly Father asks obedience until death.

You think, *Oh, well. I can't do that. Jesus did it, but I can't.* Sometimes it takes you time to digest things or store them in your brain, and then later they become a part of you. Your brain tells you what you want to do in the dark to keep hidden. Your conscience halts you. You think, *Can I do this in front of my earthly father and my heavenly Father?* Then you can decide what is right and what is wrong.

Say you don't listen to your conscience. You go ahead and do what is wrong, and self-restraint goes out the window. What are you left with? Guilt. Guilt comes with heavy baggage that can last a lifetime. Then you ask yourself, *Why did I do that? That was wrong. Why didn't I listen to my heavenly Father?*

Eric Metaxas, in his book *Seven Men and the Secret of their Greatness,* writes,

> The great criminologist James Q. Wilson says all of his studies have led to the same conclusion: Crime begins when children are not given adequate moral training, when they do not develop internal restraints on impulsive behavior.[A1] Eric Metaxas, 7 Men And The Secret of Their Greatness, (Nashvile, Tennesse: Thomas Nelson, 2013), pg.188

Remember when your parents told you not to play with matches? "You will get burned," Dad said.

You repied, "Come on, Dad. No, I won't."

Come on, Dad. Say it. Be brave. When you play with sex, you will get pregnant. That topic will open up a lot of conversation.

Let's go back to the topic of obedience. *NIV Life Application Study Bible* lists in its index under the term *obedience* sixty-six references in the scriptures. From start to finish, birth to death, God knew you would have trouble with this subject. Guess what? At the top of the list is that God does not force us to obey Him.

You are free to eat from any tree in the garden; but you must not eat from the tree of the knowledge of good and evil, for when you eat of it you shall surely die. (Genesis 2:16–17)

You are designed in a complicated way to think about good and evil. Innocence is pure. If your parents tell you not to do something but you do it anyway, you are in trouble. The Lord simply told two people not to do something that they went and did anyway, and they were in big trouble. The naked truth came out. Evil was exposed. Now you know why there are sixty-six scriptures on *obedience*.

Unlimited patience: do you have it? Do your mother and father have it? No! Jesus Christ has it!

If you take the time to read from the sixty-six scriptures on *obedience,* when you are tempted to do something negative, do you think you will read one of them before acting?

Jesus gives you His unlimited patience, but why do you test Him? You may test Him many times until finally one day you do not want to test Him anymore. How do you make your decisions about what you think is right and wrong? Compare what you want to do to the sixty-six scriptures on obedience. Does this hold up to what someone who is higher than you is trying to tell you?

Fathers, wake up! Tell your daughters to listen and care when it comes to what their heavenly Father says about childbearing.

Genesis 9:5–6 says:

> And for your lifeblood I will surely demand an accounting. I will demand an accounting from every animal. And from each man, too, I will demand an accounting for the life of his fellow man. Whoever sheds the blood of man, by man shall his Blood be shed; for in the image of God has God Made man.

To "demand an accounting" means that God will require each person to account for his or her actions. We cannot harm or kill another human being without answering to God. A penalty must be paid. Justice will be served.

God explains why murder is so wrong: to kill a person is to kill one made in God's image.

How are our children dying? Abortion, drugs, alcohol, parents killing them, suicide, lack of parental guidance, crime, drive-bys, lack of proper medical care, disease, starvation, house fires, automobile accidents, drowning, the mentally disturbed who have no business with guns, and children who have no supervision and pick up a parent's gun and shoot like it's a toy but kill someone.

There is a poem that was published by the National Library of Poetry in 1998. It was written in Tehachapi, California, for a contest. It did not win, but it is in the book[A2]:Louise Nikkel,"Listen and Care," Best Poems of 1998 The Library of Poetry, Owings Mills,MD, Watermark Press, pg.80 *f*

Listen and Care

Do you know who you are?
Or do you know who you are will make a difference?

You can make the numbers diminish by defiance.
Or when will the innocent commit or unite to compliance?
Uplift your ways, your thoughts, your cares to One whose
thoughts and cares are higher than ours, born of a virgin.

Respectfully, do you want your first born, virgin born?
Enter the next generation's health in your womb.
All of you who care closed as tight as an unopened rose bud,
when will you listen?
Let preservation of your integrity, your reputation,
Your emotions, your mind, your body, your word,
strengthen you.
Let your youth be protected, enjoyed. You who are admired
not to give yourself so freely.

Creation passes through our hands.
Are you to forgive us of what we have become?
Respect your direction don't let confusion come.
Enter the next generation's health in your womb.
All of you do you really care?

—Louise Nikkel

Do you know that who you are will make a difference? Yes.

"Put his Spirit in our hearts as a deposit" (2 Corinthians 1:22). You make a difference in how you think and where your strength comes from. You are powerful when Jesus Christ is in you. Jesus would not let Satan tempt Him because He had the power of the Holy Spirit in Him. The Holy Spirit inside of you is your power to resist temptation.

[A3]Louise Nikkel, "Today and Tomorrow,"Into The Unknown, Owings Mills, MD, Watermark Press, 1996, pg. 202.Whose character is the role you want to portray today and tomorrow?

What are the beliefs that will guide you through your life away from sorrow?

When will you choose to pour out on stationary paper your beliefs and characteristic wishes—tomorrow?

Where will you search for encouragement and the answers to your questions?

How will you find the source for your strength—through suggestions?

What tree stands firm and weathers all storms?

How will you water the tree?

Where will the wind blow the leaves?

Who finds joy, peace, love, rhythm, and harmony?

Who finds the tree of life, finds salvation, from the beginning, the Omega, today and tomorrow.

While I sat in church one Sunday at Grace Baptist in Bakersfield, California, three girls were introduced because they had a message to give to the whole congregation. They had all agreed not to become pregnant before they were married. Yes, they knew the character of the role they wanted to portray to themselves and the whole congregation.

Take a stand. Take steps that you will put on paper. Join with other young girls—young women like these three—and say, "I choose not to become pregnant before I am married." You can make that commitment, and it will make a difference in your life.

Stop right now and pray a prayer:

> Father in heaven, please instill in me the power of Your strength so that through self-control and obedience You can help me resist the temptation of sexual immorality. It is not Your plan in my life for me to have a child out of wedlock. It is not Your

plan in my life for me to have an unwanted
child. It is Your plan for me to wait until I
am married to bring a child into this world
so my husband and I can care for and love
him or her. Amen.

If we talk about a temple, we think of a building that has
a foundation that has been soundly constructed to stand
firmly in place for many years. Do you think of yourself as
God's temple?

Take time out to read what Paul is telling you in 1
Corinthians 3:16 about God's temple.

If you do not have an earthly father—if you have one who
is absent from raising you—then you still have a heavenly
Father who loves you more than you will know. He can
build in you a soundly constructed foundation to stand
firmly in place for many years.

In Bakersfield, California, I worked for a company called
Biomat Griffolds. This highly scientific plasma-donation
center taught me many lessons about the donation process of
collecting plasma. One of the screening questions was this:
"Have you had any tattoos within the last twelve months?"

"Why was that so important?" you might ask. There is
always a chance after getting a tattoo that one might get

hepatitis. A risk from unsterile tattooing can transmit the blood-borne hepatitis C virus. The foundation of our plasma to make the medication albumin depends on people who are fit and sound and keep their bodies sacred to better humankind. Just an example to keep God's temple fit.

Plan to keep a journal of your life's plans regarding how you will take care of yourself using God's temple as an example. Did you ever ask yourself, "Did God's plans fail?" We do not know all that God has in store for us. He has certainly laid a foundation to steer our foolish plans away from sorrow, if only we will listen. So keep your journal see if your plans come to fruition. Compare them to God's principles, morals, integrity, obedience, self-control, selflessness, serving, and how you are taking care of God's temple. When you can do this, there will be less impulsiveness in your life that will actually steer you away from trouble.

Not to change the subject, but on the same subject of God's plan for you and all of us, there is a song that comes to my mind. It is called "The Old Rugged Cross." There are many beautiful ornamental crosses and jewelry crosses that are manmade. Jesus died on an old rugged cross to save you from sin. Did God's plan fail? No. Do our plans fail? Yes. He gives you a choice: follow, obey, trust, believe in Him, and you will have eternal life. Jesus came lived and died to show you the way and to show you His plan works. Trouble will come, but He gives you the strength to stand up to it.

What have you learned that will call you to action? Meditate on the sixty-six scriptures of obedience. Now if you are ten, eleven, twelve, thirteen, fourteen, fifteen, sixteen, seventeen, eighteen, nineteen, or twenty to twenty-five, you have plenty of time to meditate. Start your journal today, because who you really are will make a difference to your heavenly Father, for His glory lasts to eternity.

One of the ways you can practice less impulsiveness is to control your tongue. An old Proverb says, "He who guards his lips guards his life, but he who speaks rashly will come to ruin" (Proverbs 13:3). Look at all the ways words can hurt and destroy you. There is a long list: kids at school, cyberbullying, Facebook, texting, negative comments, bullying in person, and people who are critical of everything you are not. Does it not make sense that if one can control the tongue, one can control the rest of one's body? We will discuss this more on the chapter of the trap. On the subject of control, let's see what Peter has to say.2 Peter l:6-7, "and to knowledge, self- control; and to self-control, perseverance, godliness; and to godliness, brotherly kindness; and to brotherly kindness, love." Can you see how you can have self- control over your mouth, your emotions, what you eat or what you drink?

In one week, write down how you are having trouble controlling your mouth. Then the next week, concentrate on your emotions. Are you keeping them in check? Or are you letting your emotions control you? What do you eat? Are you consuming too many hard-to-remove calories? Or are you burning unneeded calories on a regular basis? Do you see how perseverance and love take on what it takes to keep the temple of your body fit?

When it comes to alcohol, what do you drink? If you are sixteen or older to age twenty-five, you may have trouble with one drink, two drinks, three drinks, four drinks, and five drinks you may be gone. Everyone is affected differently by alcohol. Blood alcohol levels kill by poisoning you. Everyone is different when it comes to alcohol. But everyone loses self-control. A good many lose their dignity, their driver's license, their automobiles, and their lives over alcohol, or they kill another person because of a drunken state. Yet alcohol is tested over and over again by youths and adults. Why do we test it? Why do we test what we already know? Some people cannot sip it. They drink it again and again and do not know when to stop. Only self-control can tell you what you should or should not drink when it comes to alcohol. Unfortunately, not everyone has that self-control. When it comes to alcohol, do you lose your self-control?

The Trap

We have talked about obedience and self-control. Now it is time to talk about the trap. The trap involves steps taken before and after that bring consequences. The simplest example is the hunter who takes steps to trap an animal for its fur. The consequence is that animal will try to free itself or it will die.

What are traps that we fall into? What are steps taken to make us fall into these traps? What are the consequences of how will we try to free ourselves?

One example comes to mind. A married couple in Bakersfield, California, committed themselves to helping young girls who had become pregnant to not choose abortion by helping them bring their babies into the world. The young girls wanted to free themselves of the consequences. The young married couple was successful in witnessing to these young girls and physically helping them bring their babies into the world. God bless them all.

How do you fall into such a trap? No, not me. I will not become pregnant before I am married. So how does it happen? It is selfishness, self-centeredness, pleasure, lust, lying, and curiosity, but it is not true love if there is no commitment.

At sixteen you might be thinking of going to the prom with an older boyfriend who is eighteen. The night is romantic. You are both dressed up, and you both look great. The dance is over, and you both end up at his place. Except no one is home but the two of you. Before this time, the red flag should be up. The trap is too tempting. Being alone where there is a bed is simply pleasure and lust. Believe me, commitment is not being thought about. It can happen to you, but it doesn't have to if you see it as a trap for both of you.

Now let's say you are in the workforce at eighteen or twenty years old, and you meet someone who is cute and you both like being together. He has his own apartment, and he invites you over. What are both of your intentions? Just to visit? No, you are both in the temptation trap. It is too easy for self-control to go out the window—another red flag. Can you see self-centeredness, selfishness, and pleasure happening here? Another trap, are you ready for commitment? Probably not if you just met.

Emotions and feelings are also a trap. You are overtaken by charm, blue eyes, a pleasing personality, and good looks. You are desiring a connection. There is no harm in that. Now you want to find out more. Emotions and feelings—you can let them escalate, or you can bring them down to earth. You can find out about the true person by being a friend, not by needing a sexual relationship because of emotions and feelings.

A young man isn't prepared to be put in a trap by his girlfriend who he may or may not love because she becomes pregnant. Now there is a consequence for all three parties.

It is rare for a young man to be prepared at ages sixteen to twenty-two. For a young girl, it is rare to be prepared as a teenager to bring a baby into this world as you are still learning to become an adult. For adults it is not easy, so how can it be easy for a teenager?

How does lying come into play? It is a part of the trap. Once you lie, the lie just keeps getting bigger. You can lie to your parents, you can lie to yourself, and you can lie to a sister, your brother, your grandparents, the ones you supposedly love, and your boyfriend, but the one person you cannot lie to is Jesus Christ. He will catch you in a lie every time. Then you have to deal with the consequence with Him. It may take a very long time. That is between you and the Lord Jesus Christ.

Jesus gives us scripture for you to not step into the messes you create for yourself. He was tested, and He showed you how to avoid temptation. He died for you because He loves you. How do you show Him that you love Him? Action is love. Love is action. Show Him.

Give Him the glory when you ask yourself, "Now was that the way the Lord would handle it?" Be accountable to Him, not your own selfish desires, and He will show you the way.

He is helping me write this book, not me. He is showing me the way, and I thank Him for the inspiration. Fathers, tell your daughters to write the stories of their lives and how the Lord led them away from temptation. Give Him the glory.

Meditation

Meditate on one of the sixty-six scriptures of obedience each day.

Day 1: Genesis 3:5

Imagine only knowing goodness, not evil and never being tempted. Sounds naïve. Go to God when you are tempted. He lets you know what is right, and He makes us consider the consequences.

Day 2: Genesis 3:11–13.

This pertains to choice, being deceived, blaming others, and trusting God.

Day 3: Genesis 3:14–19

This is about consequences, punishment, disobedience, forgiveness, and restoration.

Day 4: Genesis 17:1

The Lord appears to Abram and asks him to be blameless.

Day 5: Genesis 19:16

Moses tells us a true story of hesitation to obey.

Day 6: Genesis 22:3

To understand this test of obedience, you will have to start at Genesis 22:1–18.

Day 7: Exodus 1:17–21

There are certain situations where you should not obey authority when it means disobeying God.

Day 8: Exodus 5:4–9

There are those situations where you will suffer for doing what is right, but God will not desert you

Day 9: Exodus 6:10–12

The key is obeying with "persistent faith" when all the odds are against you, like how Samaritan Purse serves all over the world. Samaritan's Purse is an evangelical Christian humanitarian aid organization to people in physical need as a key part in Christian ministry. Founded by Bob Pierce in 1970. Franklin Graham became president in 1979. Headquarters are in Charlotte and North Wilkesboro, North Carolina.

Day 10: Exodus 8:25–29

Obeying halfway is not fully obeying.

Day 11: Exodus 15:26

It is extremely important to read not only the verse, but the application note explains this verse says how Gods moral laws keep us from diseases.

Day 12: Exodus 16:45

This is a perfect example how God tests our obedience.

Day 13: Leviticus 9:22–23

To understand this scripture, you need to read Leviticus 9:6. Then you may want to read all of chapter 9, and be sure to read the footnotes. The key is following and serving daily.

Day 14: Leviticus 10:2

To understand this verse, please read the footnotes for 10:1 and 10:2. This is a lesson in obedience even though today we do not have burnt offerings.

Day 15: Numbers 2:34

Imagine 603,550 Israelites doing what they were told by the Lord and Moses. Be sure to read the footnote.

Day 16: Numbers 14:40–44

This verse definitely gives you something to think about. If you make the time today, read starting verses 20 through 45 and the footnotes from 14:20–44. (The Lord knows what is in your heart.)

Day 17: Deuteronomy 30:11–14

You will love this one. "No, the word is very near you; it is in your mouth and in your heart so you may obey it."

Day 18: Joshua 1:6–8

This is definitely a must to understand who you are will make a difference to the Lord.

Day 19: Joshua 3:13–14

This is about following instructions and trust.

Day 20: Joshua 9:1–6

Three words come into play here: "opposition, deception, and wisdom. Be sure to read the footnote to understand.

Day 21: 2 Chronicles 18:15–16

This talks about lying to make ourselves look good. To understand it would be very helpful to read the whole story starting at chapter 18

Day 22: Joshua 11:15

The key here is that you can control your choice to obey. Be sure to read the footnote to grasp the entire meaning.

Day 23: Joshua 22:5

This is a clear, simple, important message to love and obey.

Day 24: Judges 6:37–39

The truth of this message is not to ask for signs from God. He has already given you guidance through His word. Be sure to read the footnotes for 6:37–39 and 6:39. Meditate on this today.

Day 25: 1 Samuel 3:11–13

Obedience means patience. Often your timing is not God's timing.

Day 26: 1 Samuel 15:9

Selective obedience is doing things our way, and it is still disobedience. Read on footnote 15:9 for the whole story.

Day 27: 1 Samuel 15:22–23

This is a true example of God knowing what is in our hearts. A ritual carried out without truly loving God is not what God wants, and the footnote backs up this with several scriptures.

Day 28: Romans 12:1

This verse supports what was said in 1 Samuel. Paul helps us to understand how to behave and footnote 12:1 explains other scriptures about obedience.

Day 29: 1 Samuel 31:3–4

To understand this example, you must read chapter 31 and the four different footnotes below the chapter. What dilemma can you think of that does not follow God's command in your life versus human demands? Day 30: 1 Samuel 31:13

It is a short verse about how Saul and his sons were buried. The whole summary is in the footnote 31:13 consistency and 31:13 is about building on consistency one day at a time.

Day 31: Acts 5:29

This verse is telling you your priority is to obey God. Read footnote 5:29. It sounds like what is happening currently in the United States: "conflict with the world and authorities."

Day 32: 2Chronicles 26:21

This same story of Uzziah's downfall plays out with many who have been in high places and are remembered more for their downfall than for any good they did. Meditate on "consistent faith" in footnote 26:21.

Day 33: 1 Kings 17:13–16

This story is about action in faith and obedience. Relate it to something in your life that you thought was not possible but by taking steps of faith it is possible.

Day 34: 1 Kings 19:10

Sometimes you think you are the only one experiencing a problem and self-pity comes over, you but you are not the only one. Read footnote 19:10.

Day 35: 2 Kings 5:9–15 There are three lessons learned here so read footnote 9-15 about how your Father knows best, your Father wants your obedience and how God comes through.

Day 36: 2 Kings 23:4–8

By just reading the story of King Josiah in 4–8, you need to go back to 22:11 when King Josiah found out what was written in the Book of the Law: "Our fathers have not obeyed the words of this book." (Read footnote 23:4–8 to understand.) Josiah realized how bad the corruption of Judah had become, and he did something about it. When you see corruption, will you act out of obedience?

Day 37: 2 Kings 23:25

This sums up how King Josiah was remembered. Obedience, trust, and faith—is that how you would like to be remembered? Please see footnote 23:25.

Day 38: 1Chronicles 15:13–15

This short verse describes a situation where God had given specific instructions to the Levites, and they did not follow God's instructions. See footnote 15:13–15 for the full explanation. Parents love it when children learn this very important lesson.

Day 39: 2Chronicles 14:1–6

Yes, this a wonderful verse because it talks about peace. As always, see footnote 14:1–6.

Day 40: 2 Chronicles 24:5

Learning obedience is hard. A parent may say, "Do it now," but you don't listen. Here we see the Levites did not obey right away.

Day 41: 2 Chronicles 25: 2

This is sort of like bending the rules and doing something halfway. See how King Amaziah of Judah handled things.

Day 42: Philemon 1:8–9

A story about a conflict between two friends and how commitment of obedience is the best answer.

Day 43: Hosea 1:2–3

This is a difficult verse to understand. You will need to read the whole footnote to grasp the entire meaning Obedience may seem difficult, but God "requires extraordinary obedience" because He knows we "face extraordinary times" as we have in our past and continue to do so.

Day 44: Jonah 1:3

This is a prime example of someone who thought he could run from God. Please see the lesson God has to teach you in footnote l:3 and 1:3. Yes, there are two footnotes here. Both are important

Day 45: Matthew 1:24

How easy would it be for the angel of the Lord to come and tell you, "This is what I want you to do," and you obey God regardless of what other people say. That is exactly what Joseph did. He obeyed and made Mary his wife.

Day 46: Matthew 3:10

This is a very short verse with a whole lot of meaning. This calls for "action in obedience" to be "productive" for serving God.

Day 47: Matthew 4:1

Jesus in the desert resists temptation. As you read footnote 4:1, relate to how you can overcome temptation. The second 4:1 talks about the reality of Satan. The third 4:1ff talks about showing us how human Jesus was. The fourth 4:1ff shows us how when we are tired, alone, and hungry, how "vulnerable" we can be. In 4:1–10, read the three issues here everyone struggles over.

Day 48: Matthew 4:3–4

It is so important to apply this message to your heart. It is explained clearly in footnotes 4:3–4. You all have desires, but Jesus "shows you the right way and the right time" take time on this passage. You may want to meditate longer on it.

Day 49: Luke 4:1–13

Satan tries to tempt you because he wants to be powerful! Do not let him. God is more powerful. His word can lead you away from temptation, just as Jesus resisted Satan in the desert. Read all the footnotes here, starting with 4:1–13.

Day 50: Matthew 5:20

Look at your heart and see where your true allegiance lies. Jesus is explaining about the law. See in the second footnote 5:20 the four points that are discussed.

Day 51: Matthew 23:23–24

This verse is about following the letter of the law in one area but not giving of yourself and your time in helping others. See 23:23,24footnote and 23:: 24 footnote Jesus is condemning the teachers of the law.

Day 52: Matthew 26: 37–38

It is hard to imagine that night when Jesus went with Peter and two other men to pray in Gethsemane. He knew the pain of all sins being laid on Him, and He knew what His Father was asking him to do. The only way He was going to get through this was the strength He received from His heavenly Father, the same way you can have that strength.

Day 53: Mark: 4: 24-25

Understanding God's instruction and applying His word to your life helps you to grow and to obey. Refer to the beginning of chapter 4 to understand the story of the parables.

Day 54: Luke 1:38

The best way to explain this verse is "willing acceptance." An angel came to Mary, and she accepted what the angel told her and agreed to be the mother of Jesus. What a calling!

Day 55: Luke 17:7–10

To understand this passage, you will have to read the footnote that talks about how obedience, "is our duty."

Day 56: John 14:21

This is beautiful verse that is well understood, Jesus simply says, "Whoever has my commands and obeys them, he is the one who loves me."

Day 57: Romans 1:1

Paul sets the example to be a servant to be obedient and completely dependent on Christ. Paul turned himself around from persecuting Christians to being used by God to spread the gospel. You too can turn yourself toward God and be completely dependent on Him. Read 1:1 three times to understand the background in the footnote.

Day 58: Romans 5:20

This is a short verse that needs more explaining. Go back to 5:12. Read through to 20, and also footnote 5:20 gives the example of climbing a ladder (imagine climbing a cell phone tower ladder). It seems impossible, but with God's power, He lifts you up.

Day 59: Romans 6: 17

When you think about God's power fully, you think about following Him with your whole heart. In footnote 6:17, it asks the question, "How do you rate your heart's obedience?"

Day 60: Romans 13:1

This verse is so helpful for all time because it explains about submitting to "governing authorities." Then in footnote 13:1 it states, "We should never allow government to force us to disobey God." Can you imagine that on the headlines of your local newspaper? Would that solve some of the problems we have today? Can you stand up and say, "No one will ever make me disobey God"? Romans 13:1–6 and footnotes 13:1 and 13:1ff are a must to read and understand.

Day 61 Ephesians 6:1–2

This is a particularly special verse. Please include up to verse 4: "Fathers, do not exasperate your children; instead, bring them up in the training and instruction of the Lord." It is extremely important to read footnote 6:1–2 and 6:1–4. Learn the difference between obeying and honoring. Not everyone grows up with an earthly father present. They leave or are out of the picture completely. How desperately important it is for you to know how much your heavenly Father loves you.

Day 62 Philippians 2:12

This is an excellent verse on how not to become sidetracked when you are on your own. Remember to take God with you. He is your strength and encouragement. In the footnote 2:12, it explains that Paul was not there to remind the Philippians about obedience. When a strong Christian mentor in your life is far away or dies, you must cling to Christ.

Day 63: Hebrews 5:8

Jesus "chose freely" to obey God and gave Himself as an example for you to follow today. As always, read footnote 5:8.

Day 64: Hebrews 11:7

The importance of this verse talks about believing without seeing, like in Noah's case, who had complete faith and trust and obedience in his heart. God gave Noah strength, God will give you strength. See footnote 11:7.

Day 65: 1 John 2:6

"Who claims to live in him must walk as Jesus did." Obey what Jesus taught you by following His example to love one another.

Day 66Genesis 2: 16-17

As it was stated in the very beginning in Genesis 2:16–17, God gives us a choice "with rewards" and "consequences if we disobey." What will you choose? Write your own story. Take God with you, and give Him all the glory.

Personalities of Different Men

·······◇·◇·◆◇·◇·◇·◇·······

In the parables Jesus teaches us through short stories using "physical symbols to illustrate spiritual truths" (Luke 8:9–16 NIV). This is how a father can start out talking with his daughter about the "secrets of the kingdom of God," and how the symbol of the seed is the true word of God.

In order not to be led astray from the mischievous hearts of men, a father can gradually help his daughter to understand men's motives. Don't all fathers feel a lifelong protection for their daughters? They feel it in the beginning when they are babes but also when they are older, they can become rebellious and very strong-willed. How easy it is to go astray unless young girls have fathers who are willing to spend time with them building a strong foundation of God's principles. Don't think you can leave it all up to the mother of your daughter. Young girls need your input, your male instinct that God gave you to shape through scripture strength in the heart and mind of your daughter.

The controller is a man who will try to control every aspect of your life. In *Webster's Encyclopedic* Unabridged Dictionary of the English Language, Avenel, New Jersey, Random House Value Publishing 1986, pg.318 controller is defined as, "1. Exercise restraint or direction over; dominate; command. 2. to hold in check; curb: to control a horse; to control one's emotions. 4. To eliminate or prevent the flourishing or spread." I think you get the point. There are plenty of them out there. The abuser falls into this category. He most likely was abused when he was a child, and to exercise control, he will beat up on you. The whole idea is to complement one another. A man and woman are to have each other's best interest at heart. Violence does not solve anything but brings trouble and ugly consequences. There is also the power seeker. He is related to the controller. However, the power seeker likes to be on top of his company, on top in politics. He can be a workaholic. He wants to be on top in entertainment. He likes having a companion but has little time for you. Now if you are the same way, you may get along just fine or not at all eventually.

Then there is the cheater. How do you know he will become a cheater? This is more difficult to talk about. When one marries too early in life, like a teenager or in the early twenties, personalities change so often. There are always exceptions to this rule. Some young people truly find lifelong relationships and believe in faithfulness and really enjoy being together. They are the smart ones. One morning you wake up and find out your spouse is dating someone else. Why? There can be two reasons—you are not doing something he wants, or you are doing something he does not like, for starters. He does not discuss it with you. He just goes looking for someone else.

Compulsive men like things done a certain way to relieve their anxiety and stress. *Webster's Encyclopedic Unabridged Dictionary of the English Language, Avenel, New Jersey, Random House Value Publishing, copyright 1986, pg. 303,* says compulsive means, "governed by an obsessive need to conform; behavior driven by a compulsion." Of course, girls and women can be this way too. Can you imagine two people living under the same roof with these problems? There is always compromise.

Money

Parenting, on how boys and girls grow up, some are good money managers and some are not, just like there are good listeners and bad listeners because some parents talk too much. Money management must be taught from an early stage in life and progressed to adulthood. Now if it is not your gift or you were not taught, don't feel bad. Just go to the experts. There are plenty of books on financial literacy. You must do the research on how to manage money. Just be a researcher, or get her a tutor if she stumbles in math. Include your daughter at an early age in conversations about debt, budgets, controlled spending, not having to have everything she wants, etc. Exercise self-control on spending and using credit. Let her know electricity costs money. Let her see your monthly bill for electricity. Maybe she will turn her lights off in her room. There does not have to be naivety early in life so that there is a rude awakening during the teenage years and early twenties in regard, to money management. We start out with building blocks in kindergarten. Why not money management blocks for our kids with fathers teaching daughters? Maybe many of you do. Why is the United States in so much debt? Fathers, daughters, mothers, sons, politicians, grandfathers, grandmothers—why are we not teaching more about money management?

Marriage

"Do not plow with an ox and a donkey yoked together." (See below)

Let us give credit where credit is due. Who said this, and what does it mean? Imagine explaining this to your ten-year-old daughter. If she grew up on a ranch, she might know exactly what it means.

First ask your daughter to figure it out for herself. Applaud her if she points out that an ox and a donkey are of different strength and weight or size and cannot pull a plow evenly.

This is sort of like Republicans and Democrats who cannot compromise to meet needs of the American people. The personality of some are like an ox, and some are like donkeys. Some people are savers and planners, some are spenders and non-planners.

"Do not plow with an ox and a donkey yoked together." Does she know who said this? Moses! His advice still stands today. Where is it found? Deuteronomy 22: 10,New Application Study Bible Wheaton,Illinois, Tyndale House Publishers,copyright 1994, pg. 310 Why did he say this? In order to protect us.

The same goes for marriage. When you decide to become yoked together in marriage, remember, plowing a course will not be even but difficult. It is just like those who sew know two kinds of different thread should not be sewed together, for they wear uneven and wash differently. When differences flare up—and they will—compromise and devotion come into play.

Dad, give an example of compromise. First let us define it. *Webster's Encyclopedic Unabridged Dictionaryof the English Language, Avenel,New Jersey, Random House Value Publishing, copyright 1994,pg.303,* says, "1. A. settlement of differences by mutual concessions; an agreement reached by adjustment of conflicting or opposing claims, etc." It's like something in the middle between different things. The best example is sports. Now either you like to play sports or you like to be a spectator. Most men like both. However, some girls or women like to play sports but they are not spectators. They do not like to watch football, baseball, basketball, or golf on TV. (Those who do praise God for the men.) For the ladies who don't, that can be a problem, for most men do like watching sports on TV. If as a girl you learn some of the rules of the games and like going to games with your husband, that can surely be helpful. If you do not, that can cause a wedge in your marriage. Then you hope you both can find something in common you both enjoy doing.

Dad let us pick up where we left off, on the subject of marriage. And Dad, let's keep it simple. Remember I am only ten.

Keeping it simple, we need help! Let's go to *Webster's*

Dictionary. Let us look up the word and you read it out loud. The first word is *emotion:* "I. An affective state of consciousness in which joy, sorrow, fear, or the like, is experienced."Webster's Encyclopedic Unabridged Dictionary of the English Language, Avenel New Jersey, Random House Value Publishing,copyright 1986, pg.467.

Okay, stop right there. That is what marriage is like! Over the course of time in a marriage, many emotions take place because a woman goes through different emotions than a man and a man goes through different emotions than a woman.

However, before marriage over the course of time, our emotions change. The emotions that you have today at ten will change by the time you reach sixteen, and at twenty, twenty-five, and thirty and so on. It is the same in a young boy at ten, sixteen, twenty-five, thirty, and so on.

Emotion is not devotion. That is our next word to look up.

Okay, Dad, devotion is sounding like church.

Read it out loud!

Devotion is defined as "l. "Profound dedication" #2. Earnest attachment to a cause, person,"Webster's Encyclopedic Unabridged Dictionary of the English Language, Avenel,New Jersey, Random House Value Publishing, 1986, pg. 395. Wait, define profound.

Dad, I cannot. I know, look it up. "Profound entering deeply into subjects of thought or knowledge. Intense; extreme profound anxiety."Webster's Encyclopedic Unabridged Dictionary, Avenel,New Jersey, Random House Value Publishing, copyright 1986, pg.1149

Wait! This is what marriage can be like—two people with two different views can bring extreme anxiety.

Dad, the other definitions in *Webster's* say, "3 profound means being or going far beneath what is superficial, external, or obvious: profound insight. 4. Of deep meaning; of great and broadly inclusive significance: A profound book. 5. Extending, situated, or originating far beneath the surface: the profound depths of the ocean." Dad, I understand number three the best.

Exactly—marriage is not superficial, and it is not just looking at the exterior of blue eyes. It is not obvious, and it requires much thought. It is like a realization that you daily express love and devotion. Marriage works when you live in the desire of the highest form of devotion, respect, credibility, and trust.

Thanks, Dad, for taking time to explain these things. I love you so much.

Thank You, heavenly Father, for inspired scriptures on the teachings of obedience. I love You so much.

About the Author

Louise Brunner, a native of Houston, was raised around the Texas Medical Center, which she watched built from the ground up. She developed a love for the medical field and entered the surgical technician training program in Wichita Falls, Texas, compliments of the Air Force in 1970. She was stationed at Keesler Air Force Base in Biloxi, Mississippi, and trained to assist in delivering babies, orthopedic surgery, and general surgery. She went on to earn an associate's degree from Bakersfield College and retired as a registered nurse after many years. She attends Oakwood Baptist Church, sings in the choir, and has been married to her husband more than eighteen years.

Printed in the United States
By Bookmasters